For such a small city, Pasadena is exceptionally rich in art and culture, with museums and galleries all over town. Many of these take part in Pasadena's free, twice-annual Art Night. Shown here are the Norton Simon, USC Pacific Asia Museum, Armory Center for the Arts, Kidspace, the Pasadena Museum of California Art, and The Huntington

The Norton Simon Museum houses one of the world's most remarkable private art collections, assembled over many decades by the late industrialist and philanthropist Norton Simon. Known for works by such masters as Cézanne, Van Gogh, Rembrandt, and Degas, the museum also has a stunning collection of Japanese woodblock prints, a rich array of Asian art, and significant contemporary pieces. The sculpture garden is particularly impressive, and it includes the bronze piece depicted here by Henry Moore, titled King and Queen.

Norton Simon Museum, 411 West Colorado Boulevard, Pasadena

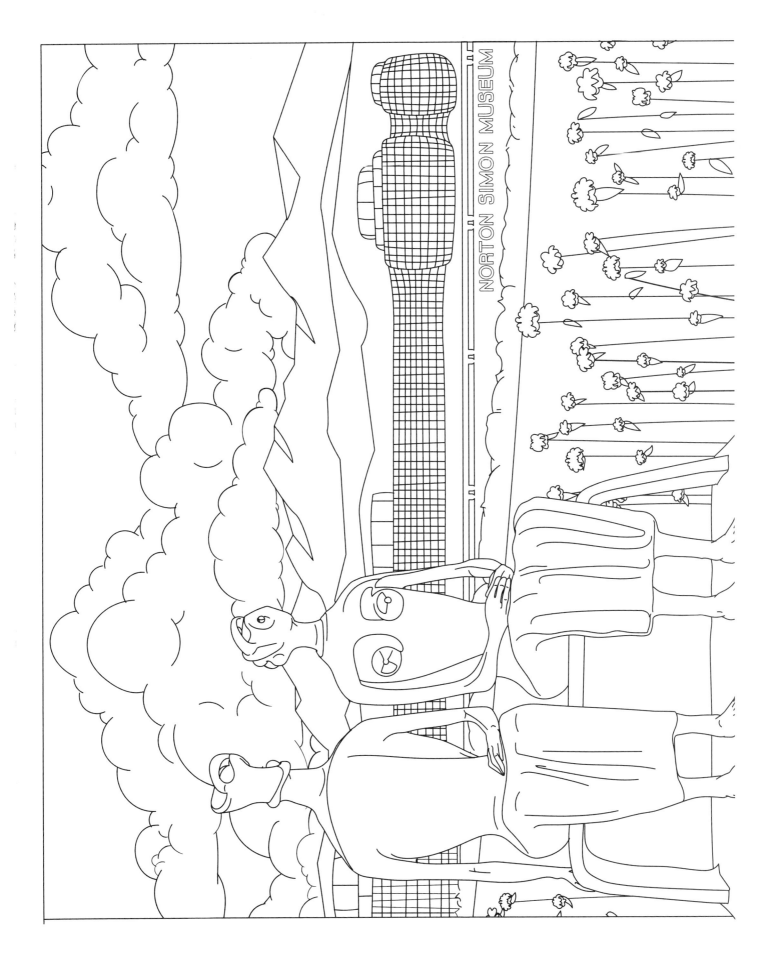

Founded in 1919 by Henry E. Huntington, The Huntington Library is an internationally renowned research and educational institution that houses more than seven million items, including 400,000 rare books and one million photographs and prints. Two of the best-known works in The Huntington's European art collection include Thomas Gainsborough's *The Blue Boy* and Thomas Lawrence's *Pinkie*, famously hung opposite one another.

The Huntington Library & Botanical Gardens, 1151 Oxford Street, San Marino

Part of The Huntington Library, The Huntington Botanical Gardens are internationally famed for their array of gardens that cover about 120 acres. Some of our favorite spots at The Huntington are the Japanese Garden, the Rose Garden, the Desert Garden, and the most recent addition, the Garden of Flowering Fragrance, designed in the style of traditional Chinese scholar gardens.

The Huntington Botanical Gardens, 1151 Oxford Street, San Marino

The magnolia flower is one of the hummingbird's favorite snacks, because the pollen is rich in protein and nutrients. You can find these traditionally white flowers spread around many homes in Pasadena, as well as at the Arboretum and The Huntington Gardens. Keep an eye out — while rare, some magnolia flowers are pink, yellow, purple, or even green!

Fork-tailed bush Katydid

Black-chinned hummingbird

Harlequin bug

Pasadena is home to an impressive collection of educational institutions, including Fuller Theological Seminary, Pasadena City College, California Institute of Technology (Caltech), and Art Center College of Design. Pasadena also reputedly has the highest percentage of private schools per capita in the country, as well as a few nationally ranked public schools—and the neighboring small towns of La Cañada, South Pasadena, San Marino, and Arcadia are all famed for their public schools.

Pasadena's Playhouse District has many public art installations, including decorative crosswalks. This pattern is part of the *Moon Walk* series by artist Cynthia Luna, inspired by the art deco architecture found in Old Pasadena and around town.

East Union Street and South Oakland Avenue, Pasadena

The distinctive purple flowers of the jacaranda tree have been in the Los Angeles area for more than 100 years, and they're a sight to behold when they bloom, which is only a couple of times a year. They're located throughout Pasadena and South Pasadena, but our favorite place to see them in action is along Del Mar Boulevard between Lake and Marengo, lovingly referred to by locals as Jacaranda Row.

Carpenter bee

Ten lined June feetle

Did you know that the cheeseburger was invented in Pasadena? And that the city has the most restaurants per capita in the entire country? A must-taste destination for foodies, the Crown City (Pasadena's official nickname) has an eclectic mix of delicious, diverse eats from all over the world. Just a few of our favorites can be seen in this image, including Julienne, Lincoln, Pie 'n Burger, Daisy Mint, and Euro Pane.

A Pasadena favorite, Little Flower is a breakfast-and-lunch café, bakery, and candy kitchen. It's one of our favorite spots to meet friends for a salad or quiche and a great cup of coffee — and we always bring home a bag of their famous sea salt caramels.

Little Flower, 1422 West Colorado Boulevard, Pasadena

On almost every day of the week, you can find a farmers' market somewhere in or around Pasadena. Victory Park, South Pasadena, and Old Pasadena host some of our favorite markets, but you can also pick up fresh, organic, and locally grown produce, prepared foods, and flowers from Altadena to Montrose.

This pattern is inspired by the iron tree grates at the base of many trees lining the streets of Old Town Pasadena. These art deco-style grates are both decorative and functional; they help prevent tree roots from interfering with walkways.

A favorite of bees, bugs, and birds alike, the Angel's Trumpet (known as brugmansia) is an elegant, fragrant flower with a sweet scent of almond and citrus. They can be found blooming at The Huntington Botanical Gardens and are planted all across Pasadena and South Pasadena.

multicolored Asian ladybug

grasshopper

great basin fence lizard

One of Southern California's most famous landmarks, the Rose Bowl has been home to the New Year's Day Rose Bowl Game since 1923. As the eleventh-largest stadium in the country, the Rose Bowl also hosts concerts, soccer games, and, on the second Sunday of each month, a great flea market. Adjacent to the Rose Bowl is Brookside Golf Course, a lovely public course, as well as the Rose Bowl Aquatics Center, built for the 1984 Olympics. Walking the 5K loop around the Rose Bowl and the golf course is a regular ritual for many Pasadenans and their dogs.

The Rose Bowl, 1001 Rose Bowl Drive (off Rosemont), Pasadena

This image is based on a *Los Angeles Times* photo of the 1940 Rose Parade, featuring the original Tournament of Roses logo. The parade has been a Pasadena staple since 1890, known for its marching bands, horses, and elaborate floats covered in flowers. Enjoyed by millions around the world on TV and about a million people in person, the parade is traditionally held on New Year's Day, unless it happens to fall on a Sunday, in which case it is held on January 2nd.

As one of the many traditions of the Tournament of Roses Parade, each year one young lady from the greater Pasadena area is given the coveted title of Rose Queen. The Royal Court, made up of the Rose Queen and six Rose Princesses, rides on a special float during the parade and serves all year long as ambassadors for the Tournament of Roses. Depicted here is 1935 Rose Queen Muriel Cowan sitting atop her float, covered (as is traditional) in roses.

Muriel Cowan

1935

Roses are prominent in Pasadena's history, culture, and aesthetic—one of the city's nicknames is the Rose City, and for good reason! From the Rose Bowl to the Rose Parade, Pasadena's official flower is everywhere, including at Arlington Garden, Descanso Garden, Lacy Park, and The Huntington Gardens.

Another example of the Playhouse District's public art installations, this rose pattern is also part of *Moon Walk*, artist Cynthia Luna's series of creative crosswalk designs. Fittingly, it references the abundance of roses seen all over Pasadena, not to mention in the city's most famous parade.

El Molino Avenue and East Colorado Boulevard, Pasadena

Inspired by Lacy Park, this art nouveau rose reflects one of the prominent styles popular when the park opened in 1925. Lacy Park is home to a lush rose garden, as well as walking loops, picnic areas, and a great playground for the kids.

Lacy Park, 1485 Virginia Road, San Marino

This koi pond pattern is inspired by one of Pasadena's greatest hidden treasures: the Storrier Stearns Japanese Garden. Only open to the public on Thursdays and the last Sunday of the month, this authentic Japanese garden and teahouse are a favorite location for private events and weddings. If you tour the grounds, make sure to check out all the lovely bridges, ponds, and, our favorite, the fifteen-foot waterfall.

Storrier Stearns Japanese Garden, 270 Arlington Drive, Pasadena

Found just east of Pasadena in Arcadia, the Los Angeles County Arboretum and Botanic Garden – called the Arboretum for short – contains 127 acres of geographically grouped landscapes, including gardens from South America, the Mediterranean, and Australia. It's also famed for the flock of more than 200 peafowl that live in and around the Arboretum – much to the dismay of many nearby residents, who have to cope with their mess, noise, and the occasion attacking of cars.

Los Angeles County Arboretum and Botanic Garden, 301 North Baldwin Avenue, Arcadia

Indian Peafowl

Home to more than 350 trees, thousands of plants, and an abundance of small wildlife, Arlington Garden is Pasadena's only dedicated public garden, a grassroots project started on empty Caltrans land by a retired couple who lived on the edge of the lot. Make sure to check out some of our favorite spots, including the butterfly garden, the cactus collection, and the wildflower meadow—and yes, you can pick the oranges!

Arlington Garden, 275 Arlington Drive, Pasadena

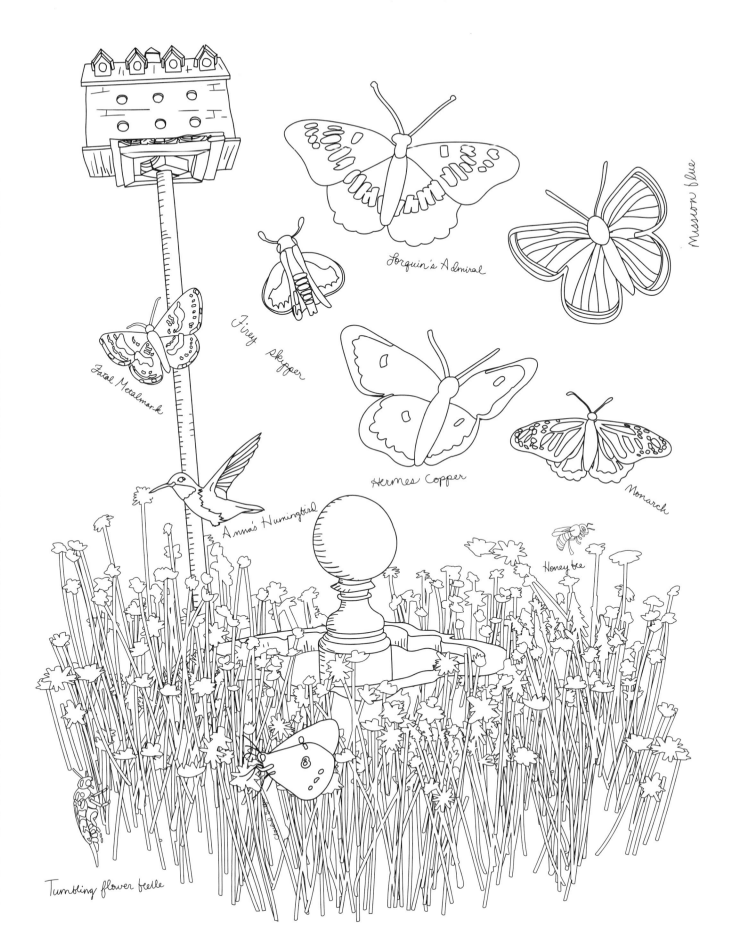

Lorquin's Admiral

Mission blue

Firey skipper

Fatal Metalmark

Hermes Copper

Monarch

Anna's Hummingbird

Honey bee

Tumbling flower beetle

The Arroyo Creek trickles through the Arroyo Seco, a natural canyon that runs from the San Gabriel Mountains south through Pasadena and into L.A. This image is from the upper Arroyo (near the Jet Propulsion Lab), a destination for hiking, biking, camping, and even fishing. Other stretches of the Arroyo are home to a casting pond, an archery range, a disc golf course, and a bird sanctuary.

Red Shouldered Hawk

Rainbow trout

Kiwi

The Enchanted Railroad Train, a beloved attraction at Descanso Gardens, is a working 1/8th-scale replica of a real diesel train. Descanso Gardens was designated a public garden in 1950, and it's home to a number of notable garden collections we love, including the International Rosarium, a bird sanctuary, and a Japanese garden and teahouse.

Descanso Gardens, 1418 Descanso Drive, La Cañada Flintridge

Ginkgo trees are known for their fan-shaped, bright-green leaves, which turn a striking yellow in the fall. Pasadena has a number of ginkgo trees all over the city, but you can most easily find them lining Colorado Boulevard in Old Town.

Pasadena's neighbor to the south is a quaint and quiet little town, with a charming downtown area known as the Mission District. Rich in quality restaurants, friendly stores, a lovely library, and a conveniently located Metro Gold Line stop, this is one spot you don't want to miss. Make sure to visit the Fair Oaks Pharmacy and Soda Fountain, Marz, the Dinosaur Farm, and Mission Wines, to name just a few of our favorites.

Mission Street between Fair Oaks and Orange Grove, South Pasadena

Historic Route 66 once ran right through Pasadena, along Colorado Boulevard and over the Colorado Bridge. It's fun to seek out the retro neon signs that are still standing from Route 66's heyday, including those at Whistle Stop Trains, the Pasada Motel, and the Hi-Way Host Motel. All three of the signs pictured are found along East Colorado Boulevard in East Pasadena.

The Doo Dah Parade began in 1978 as a free-wheeling, funny alternative to Pasadena's more famous and formal parade. Hosted annually by the Pasadena-based Light Bringer Project, the Doo Dah showcases some pretty wild characters, including the Flying Baby Naptime Aerialists, the Cupcake Cars, and the BBQ & Hibachi Marching Grill Team. Although Pasadena's Doo Dah was the first of its kind, it has since spawned copycat parades across America, including ones in Columbus, Ohio, Kalamazoo, Michigan, and Ocean City, New Jersey.

This ginkgo pattern is the third in the *Moon Walk* series by artist Cynthia Luna, and is yet another example of the decorative crosswalks seen throughout the Playhouse District. For this design, she drew her inspiration from the many ginkgo trees found along the streets of Old Pasadena.

Mentor Avenue and Colorado Boulevard, Pasadena

Beautiful bougainvillea is resplendent throughout Pasadena (especially in many residential areas). Did you know that the small white flower in the center is the actual bougainvillea flower? The colorful, paper-like petals surrounding the little flower are leaves called bract, and they can be almost any color, most commonly pink, red, orange, white, yellow, and purple.

Monarch butterfly

First opened in 1924 as a theater and acting school, the Pasadena Playhouse today produces a wide range of theatrical events, including original plays and musicals, some of which go on to Broadway. Notable players and alumni have included Dustin Hoffman, Angela Bassett, Gene Hackman, Wayne Brady, and Leonard Nimoy.

Pasadena Playhouse, 39 South El Molino Avenue, Pasadena

Vroman's is the both the largest and the oldest independent bookstore in Southern California. Established in 1894, it's a beloved Pasadena hangout that hosts hundreds of free events throughout the year; besides a broad and diverse selection of books, it holds a large newsstand (shown here), a great children's area, a stationery store, all kinds of gifts, and an excellent coffeehouse, Jones. While you're there, make sure to wave at the famous wild parrots that fly (and squawk) through the skies of Pasadena!

Vroman's Bookstore, 695 East Colorado Boulevard, Pasadena

Every summer, Levitt Pavilion hosts free concerts in Memorial Park, where families and friends of all ages bring beach chairs, blankets, and picnics to enjoy wonderful music under the stars. The range is broad: Americana, children's music, jazz, Latin, R&B, and more.

Levitt Pavilion, Memorial Park, 85 East Holly Street, Old Pasadena

Located in the heart of Old Pasadena, Castle Green is a Nationally Registered Historic Monument known for its beautiful architecture, extensive grounds, and Victorian-era furnishings. A popular filming location, Castle Green has appeared in many movies and TV shows, including *The Last Samurai* (2003), *The Prestige* (2006), *Buffy the Vampire Slayer*, *Alias*, and *CSI*. Many artists, musicians, and designers have lived or worked there, including noted contemporary American painter Kenton Nelson, whose studio was in the fabled turret for some years (he now works out of a different Pasadena studio).

Castle Green, 99 South Raymond Avenue, Old Pasadena

A neighborhood of 800-plus small Craftsman and other architecturally notable homes nestled in 12.5 acres in north Pasadena, Bungalow Heaven is one of the best collections of Arts and Crafts-era bungalows in the country. The neighborhood was Pasadena's first to be granted Landmark District status, with most of its homes built between 1905 and 1925. Back in the day, do-it-yourself bungalow kits were popular, and for less than a thousand dollars (on average, though some kits cost as much as $25,000) you could get everything necessary for building these little homes—from the framing wood to the plumbing fixtures—delivered right to your lot. These days, those kit homes are worth a far sight more than a thousand dollars!

Bungalow Heaven's boundaries are Orange Grove to the south, Washington to the north, Lake to the west, and Hill to the east.

Ernest Batchelder, the famed tile maker and a prominent figure in the Arts and Crafts movement, lived and worked out of his Pasadena home in the early twentieth century. His subtly colorful hand-crafted tiles were most commonly used around fireplaces, and they can be found in homes all over Pasadena, as well as nationwide. Batchelder was particularly fond of depicting birds, animals, and plants, and he frequently incorporated peacocks into his designs.

Built in 1908 for David Gamble of the Procter and Gamble Company, the Gamble House is one of the country's best-preserved examples of the American Arts and Crafts architectural movement. Charles and Henry Greene designed the iconic house and its furnishings, and this National Historic Landmark (run by USC) now acts as a museum. Don't miss the excellent gift shop in the adjacent carriage house.

The Gamble House, 4 Westmoreland Place, Pasadena

The Colorado Street Bridge, completed in 1913, is an architecturally significant concrete bridge spanning the enchanting Arroyo Seco, with its distinctive arches rising 150 feet above the Arroyo floor. The bridge is the site of Pasadena Heritage's annual Colorado Street Bridge Party, and it's been featured in a great many movies and TV shows, from Charlie Chaplin's *The Kid* (1921) to *Being John Malkovich* (1999), and from *Fear Factor* to *NCIS*. Its unfortunate nickname of Suicide Bridge dates back to the Great Depression, when some one hundred people reportedly jumped off the bridge.

Colorado Street Bridge is on Colorado Boulevard between Grand and San Rafael

red-shouldered hawk

lilac
crimson paint

Fox squirrel

One of Pasadena's most recognizable landmarks, Pasadena City Hall was completed in 1927. Another popular filming destination, you might recognize it as Pawnee City Hall from *Parks and Recreation*, and it was also featured in Charlie Chaplin's *The Great Dictator* (1940) and in *Beverly Hills Cop* (1984).

Pasadena City Hall, 100 North Garfield Avenue, Pasadena

PROSPECT
·PARK·
BOOKS

Published by Prospect Park Books
www.prospectparkbooks.com

Distributed by Consortium Books Sales & Distribution
www.cbsd.com

Library of Congress Cataloging in Publication Data is on file with the Library of
Congress. The following is for reference only:

Zigerelli, Ali
Color Pasadena / by Ali Zigerelli — 1st ed.
ISBN: 978-1-938849-87-9

Text by Dorie Bailey
Design & layout by Ali Zigerelli

First edition, first printing
Printed in the United States

Dorie Bailey   Ali Zigerelli